ASK ISAAC ASIMOV ?

Why are the rain forests vanishing?

Heinemann

First published in Great Britain by Heinemann Library
an imprint of Heinemann Publishers (Oxford) Ltd
Halley Court, Jordan Hill, Oxford OX2 8EJ

OXFORD LONDON EDINBURGH MADRID
ATHENS BOLOGNA PARIS MELBOURNE
SYDNEY AUCKLAND SINGAPORE TOKYO
IBADAN NAIROBI HARARE GABORONE
PORTSMOUTH NH (USA)

98 97 96 95 94

10 9 8 7 6 5 4 3 2 1

British Library Cataloguing in Publication Data is available from the British Library on request.

ISBN 0 431 07641 3

Cover designed and pages typeset by Philip Parkhouse
Printed in China

Picture Credits
pp. 2-3, © John Murray/Bruce Coleman Limited; pp. 4-5, © Fritz Prenzel/Bruce Coleman Limited;
pp. 6-7, © LaurieShock, 1992; pp. 8-9, © G. I. Bernard/NHPA; pp. 10-11, © Susan Tolonen, 1992;
pp. 12-13,© Rick Karpinski, 1992; pp. 14-15, David Austen/Bruce Coleman Limited; pp. 16-17,
© Mark Edwards/Still Pictures; pp. 18-19, © Edward Parker/Bryan and Cherry Alexander; pp. 20-21,
© Mark Edwards/Still Pictures; pp. 22-23, © Silvestris/Robert Harding Picture Library; p. 24,
© Silvestris/Robert Harding Picture Library

Cover photograph © Pictor International
Back cover photograph © Sygma/D. Kirkland

The book designer wishes to thank the models for their helpful cooperation.

Series editor: Elizabeth Kaplan
Editor: Valerie Weber
Series designer: Sabine Beaupré
Picture researcher: Diane Laska

Contents

Words that appear in the glossary are printed in **bold** the first time
they occur in the text.

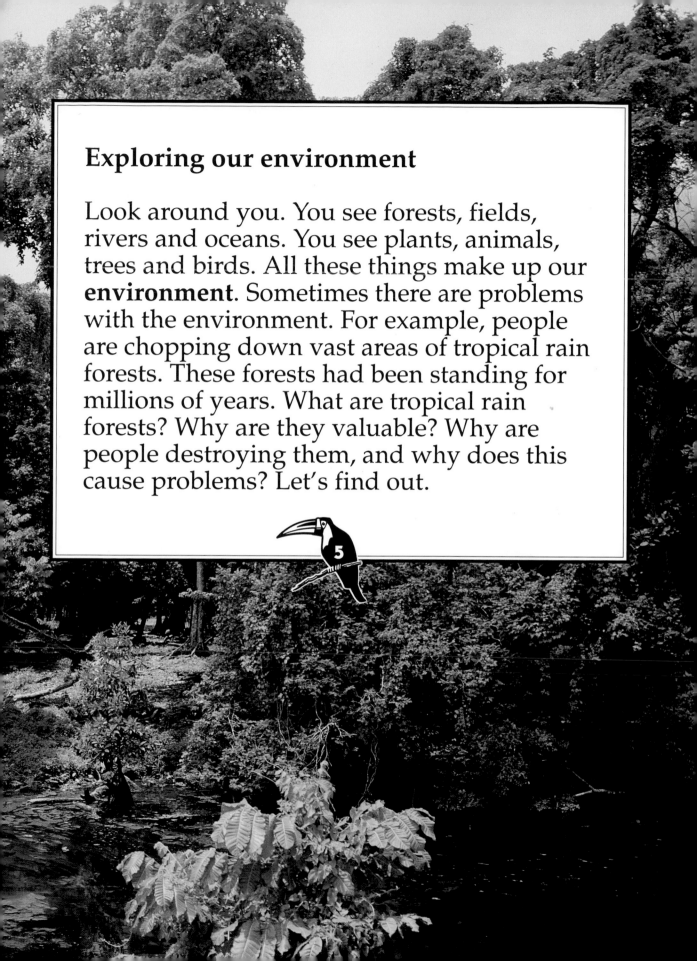

Exploring our environment

Look around you. You see forests, fields, rivers and oceans. You see plants, animals, trees and birds. All these things make up our **environment**. Sometimes there are problems with the environment. For example, people are chopping down vast areas of tropical rain forests. These forests had been standing for millions of years. What are tropical rain forests? Why are they valuable? Why are people destroying them, and why does this cause problems? Let's find out.

5

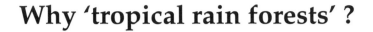

Why 'tropical rain forests' ?

Rain forests get their name from the large amounts of rain that fall on them. As much as 500 centimetres of rain can fall in one year. Only the wettest places on Earth have

North America

equator

South America

rain forests. Most of the rain forests lie in the **tropics**, as shown on the map. Find the green belt of tropical rain forests encircling the Earth at the **equator**. Rain forests also grow in other parts of the world, but this book mainly deals with tropical rain forests.

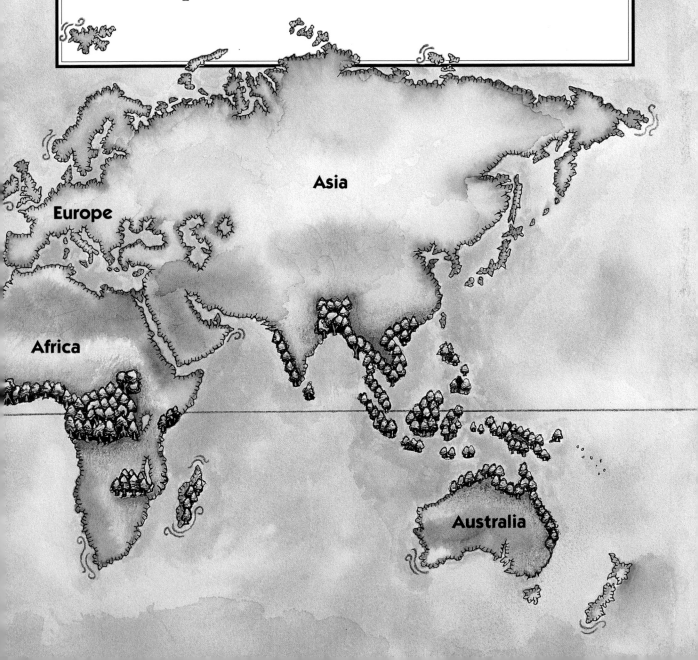

Europe

Asia

Africa

Australia

What lies under the canopy?

The heavy, steady rain that falls over the tropical rain forest supports lush plant life. Huge trees, 30 metres tall, form a leafy **canopy**. Vines twist up the trees to get more sunlight. Plants with beautiful flowers grow where tree branches divide. A few plants which grow well in shade are sprinkled across the forest floor. But thick ground-cover grows only where a lot of light gets through, for example along riverbanks or where a fallen tree has made a hole in the canopy.

9

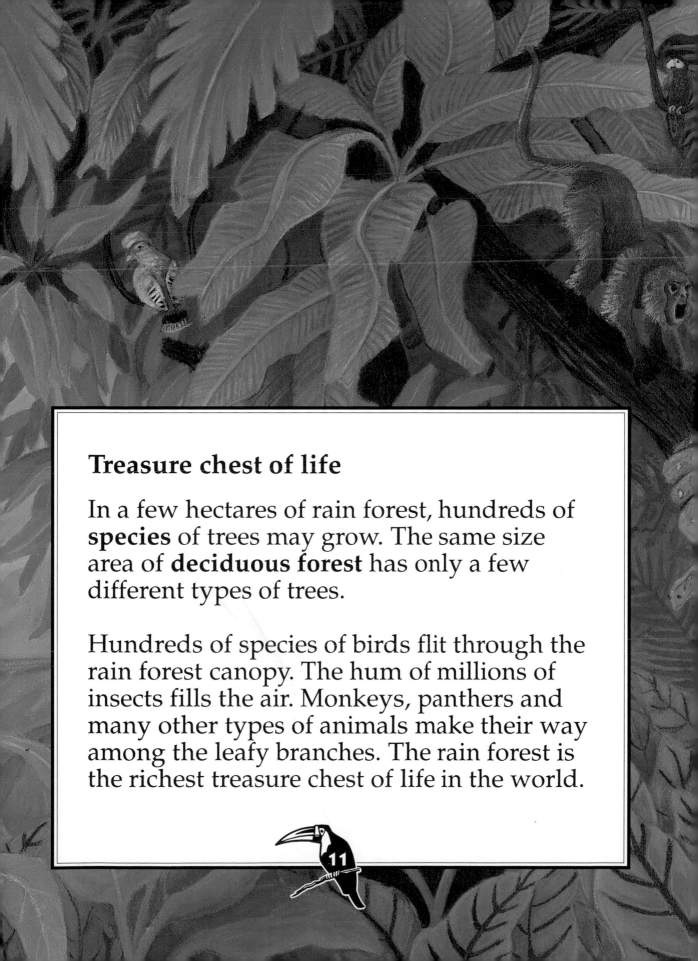

Treasure chest of life

In a few hectares of rain forest, hundreds of **species** of trees may grow. The same size area of **deciduous forest** has only a few different types of trees.

Hundreds of species of birds flit through the rain forest canopy. The hum of millions of insects fills the air. Monkeys, panthers and many other types of animals make their way among the leafy branches. The rain forest is the richest treasure chest of life in the world.

Other treasures of the rain forest

People also find treasures of plant life in the rain forest. Bananas, cinnamon, coffee and rice all grow from rain forest plants. Rain forest plants also give us medicines to fight many diseases.

Even more importantly, plants take in **carbon dioxide** and give off **oxygen**. Because plant growth is so lush there, rain forests are very important in the balancing of these gases in the **atmosphere**. Without this balance our climate would warm up. Plants and animals throughout the world would suffer.

How many rain forests have been destroyed?

Sadly, these valuable rain forests could vanish in your lifetime. In the past 30 years, more than half the world's rain forests have been destroyed, and each year even more of these lush lands disappear. People burn the forests to make farmland. They cut down the trees for lumber. They bulldoze large areas to build cattle ranches. Oil drillers in the rain forests dump **toxic wastes** on the ground and in streams. These wastes kill off plants and animals in the rain forest.

Will the rainforests grow again?

People lived in the rain forests for thousands of years without destroying them. They cleared small plots of land and planted their crops. After a few years, when the soil was no longer fertile, they abandoned their fields and the rain forest quickly grew back.

But today, people are clearing such large areas of the rain forest that the forest cannot grow back. Heavy rains quickly wash away the thin layers of soil, and the land becomes barren. The once teeming rain forest turns into a wasteland.

16

Whose fault is it?

Many people who live near the rain forests are clearing the land to make money by farming, ranching and logging. Many of the crops grown here and the beef from the ranches are shipped mainly to the United States, Canada and Europe. The lumber is made into furniture and paper and is shipped north as well.

So, we are all to blame for the destruction of the rain forest. Even if we are not the ones cutting down the trees, we use the things that come from clearing this valuable land.

How can we save the rain forests?

Most importantly, we can save them by not using products that come from cleared rain forest land. Many of the items your family buys may be made of the wood that comes from rain forest trees. Ask them not to buy these products. Use less paper and recycle what you do use. Eat less **imported** beef.

Another important thing to do is to support organizations that are trying to stop rain forest destruction. Join conservation groups that are working to **preserve** the rain forests.

21

The clock is ticking

With every second that goes by, an area of rain forest the size of a football field is destroyed! With this destruction, thousands of plant and animal species vanish. Any one of these may hold an unfound cure for cancer or other deadly disease. We cannot afford to lose the rain forests. They bring great beauty and richness to the Earth and help preserve the balance of life on our precious planet.

22

Contents

Words that appear in the glossary are printed in **bold** the first time they occur in the text.

A world of questions

Our world is full of strange and beautiful things. In some parts of the world, summer days are long and warm with plenty of sunlight. The flowers are in full bloom.

In autumn, leaves change colour and fall from the trees.

Winter days are short and cold, and sometimes snow covers the trees.

In spring, the ground warms up, flowers blossom and plants begin to grow again.

Other parts of the world have rainy and dry **seasons**. Whether a place has four seasons or just two, every region has changing seasons. Why do the seasons change? Let's find out.

What is the effect of the Earth's orbit?

Every year, the Earth orbits, or circles, the Sun once. The Earth is **tilted** at an angle as it moves along its yearly path. As it orbits the Sun, sometimes the northern half of the Earth tilts towards the Sun. At other times, the southern half of the Earth tilts towards the Sun. The part that is tilted towards the Sun receives more direct light than the part tilted away from the Sun.

Southern part of Earth tilted toward the Sun

6

Northern part of Earth tilted toward the Sun

Direct and angled light

Direct light falls straight on an object. Angled light strikes at a slant. Direct light is stronger than light that shines on an object at an angle. You can see this if you look at the cone of light made by a torch.

When the torch shines directly on an object, it strikes the object with a bright circle of light. When the rays of light strike the object at an angle, the light spreads out more. Then, the object does not look as bright. You can see how this works from the pictures on these pages.

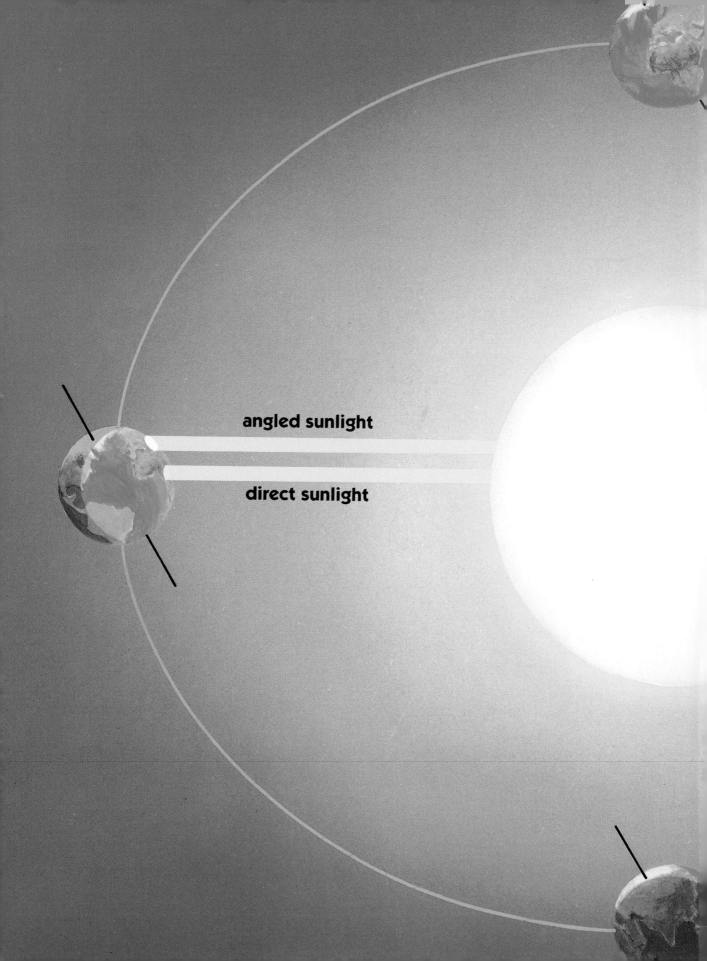

angled sunlight

direct sunlight

Why is the tilt of the Earth important?

How sunlight strikes the Earth is determined by the Earth's tilt. When the northern half of the Earth tilts *towards* the Sun, the Sun's rays hit the northern hemisphere straight on, and it is summer.

When the northern half of the Earth tilts *away from* the Sun, the Sun's rays strike the northern hemisphere at an angle, as shown. These slanting rays are not as powerful as direct rays, and it is winter.

11

Are the seasons the same everywhere?

Around the world there are not the same seasons everywhere at the same time. When it is summer on the northern part of the planet, it is winter on the southern part. When it is winter on the northern part, it is summer on the southern part.

Some parts of the Earth receive direct sunlight all year-round. These parts are near the **Equator**, the imaginary line that divides the Earth into a northern and southern half. As you go north and south of the Equator, the seasons become more dramatic.

Why do days get longer or shorter?

In summer, the Sun rises early and sets late. In winter, it rises later and sets earlier. The drawings show the times of sunrise and sunset on a summer's day and a winter's day.

In summer at the North Pole, the Sun never sets. At the time of the 'midnight sun', the Earth's tilt keeps the Pole in sunlight. The picture, taken over a few hours, shows how the Sun never dips below the horizon. In winter at the North Pole, the Sun never rises. The Earth's tilt keeps the Pole in darkness.

Sunrise and sunset in summer

4.33 a.m. sunrise

7.23 p.m. sunset

Sunrise and sunset in winter

7.22 a.m. sunrise

4.46 p.m. sunset

Why is the summer good for gardens?

Plants need sunlight and water to grow. That is why summer is the best season for our gardens. In winter, there is less sunlight and water may freeze. Many plants lie **dormant**. They look dead, but they are still alive. When spring returns, the days become longer and warmer, and the plants bud again.

Some places have dry seasons and wet seasons. In these places, plants are usually dormant in the dry season. They revive with the coming of the rains.

Hibernate, aestivate or migrate?

Some animals find it hard to live in cold weather. They lie quietly and **hibernate**, or rest, for the winter. Other animals have trouble surviving hot weather, and they rest during the summer. This is called **aestivation**. Squirrels and hedgehogs hibernate in the winter. Many animals that live in the desert aestivate during hot, dry weather.

Some animals **migrate** before winter arrives. They travel long distances from cold weather to warmer places. They usually return in spring. Many birds, including the geese and cranes shown on the right, migrate.

Seasonal celebrations

Many things depend on changing weather. Farmers plant their crops in spring because it is the time when seeds grow best. Plants grow during the warm summer months. Crops are **harvested** in autumn, just before the cold winter sets in.

Many holidays and festivals relate to the seasons. In many Western countries, Easter and Passover announce the arrival of spring. In Japan, the Snow Festival celebrates the beauty of snow. Sri Lanka and India have special festivals at the end of the rainy season.

How can you spot a new season?

Keeping track of the seasons is fun! You might notice ice melting on the footpath or the sweet scent of daffodils blooming in spring. You might hear the sound of crisp leaves blowing in the autumn wind. Wherever you live, knowing the signs of the changing seasons will help you enjoy the world around you.

Glossary

aestivation: sleeping or remaining inactive for a long period of time in summer

dormant: to be in a state of sleep or inactivity

Equator: an imaginary line that runs round the Earth's centre in an east–west direction. The Equator is halfway between the North and South Poles.

harvest: to gather in a crop which is ripe or ready for use

hibernate: to sleep or remain inactive for a long period of time during winter

migrate: to move from one place to another in search of food or warm weather

season: one of the parts into which a year is divided based on the position of the Earth in relation to the Sun

tilt: to lean or slant to one side

Index